6 Decisions

That Will Change Your Life

Leader Guide

6 Decisions
That Will Change Your Life

Participant Workbook
DVD
Leader Guide

6 Things
We Should Know About God

Participant Workbook
DVD
Leader Guide

6 Ways
We Encounter God

Participant Workbook
DVD
Leader Guide

6 Decisions

That Will Change Your Life

Leader Guide

Tom Berlin

with Justin Lucas

Abingdon Press
Nashville

Six Decisions That Will Change Your Life
Leader Guide

Tom Berlin with Justin Lucas

ISBN 978-1-426-79446-9

14 15 16 17 18 19 20 21 22 23—10 9 8 7 6 5 4 3 2 1
MANUFACTURED IN THE UNITED STATES OF AMERICA

Contents

Introduction. 7
How to Use This Leader Guide 9

1. The Decision to Follow. 13
2. The Decision for a New Life 21
3. The Decision to Mature. 29
4. The Decision to Respond 37
5. The Decision to Persevere. 45
6. The Decision to Surrender 53

Introduction

Six Decisions That Will Change Your Life is a six-week small group experience that gives participants an opportunity to learn about decisions that enable people to discern God's will and discuss the ways they are encountering God in their daily lives. The group will meet weekly to watch a video and complete Scripture study that will describe habits essential to hearing God's call and will provide new perspectives on how God communicates with us. The common goal of the Participant Workbook, DVD, and this Leader Guide is to provide an opportunity to consider God's calling in our lives and how we can faithfully respond to the Holy Spirit for decisions small and large.

Covenant Formation

It is important that each group function out of a set of shared values. Coming to a consensus or a "covenant" about what group members can anticipate from their small group will help set a tone of trust and mutuality. It is important that each member knows the small group is a safe environment to share personal information. You are encouraged to make confidentiality a part of your group covenant.

How to Use This Leader Guide

Each group will meet for six weeks for the purpose of discussing and putting into practice lessons learned during the week from the Participant Workbook. Your group can tailor the activities and discussion to the time available, usually ranging from 60 to 90 minutes with the majority of that time spent in small group discussion.

The session format described in this guide is designed to aid you as leader and facilitator and to help guide the small group experience. Sessions are easily adaptable for groups that meet for varying lengths of time. Leaders can use the sessions as they are written or choose from among the various components offered, as described below.

Preparing

A brief summary is provided at the beginning of each session so you can begin with an overview and understanding of the main goal of each week's lesson. Knowing the intended goal for the session will enable you to pick questions and manage your time within the small group to be sure the main points are discussed.

Icebreakers and Conversation Starters

Opener options have been included for each session. These activities and conversation starters help your group members connect in a fun, informal manner before entering a time of more personal and reflective sharing. Choose only one activity from the options offered. If your group meets for less than 90 minutes, you may opt to use an opener activity in the first week only, when group members may be meeting for the first time, then forgo openers in the weeks after.

The activities that are included relate in some way to the imagery used in the video or discussion topic, but you are certainly free to select what you think will work best for your group, and you may opt for an alternative opener of your own choosing.

Logistics and Covenant ✓

At your first group meeting, you may want to take time to share important logistical information relevant to your group. This may encompass things such as parking, childcare concerns, start time, discussion format, shared leadership roles, cell-phone usage, refreshments, and potential scheduling conflicts.

This is also the time to form and agree on a group covenant: a set of guidelines for behavior in the sessions and mutual promises to respect one another, listen to one another, and treat personal information shared in the group as confidential.

Workbook Review

Encourage group members to bring their Participant Workbooks to each meeting. Each session includes an opportunity for them to share reflections and insights gained from reading the workbook, studying the Scriptures, and writing down their thoughts.

Your group will find that responding to the daily readings and workbook questions will greatly enhance their experience in this study and enrich the group session. Though some group members may not be keeping up in the Participant Workbook, you'll want to include this review portion of the session for those who are doing it. Allowing this time for sharing will not only reinforce those who are practicing this discipline but will also allow others to benefit from other group members' insights and experiences.

Show DVD Video

The DVD includes a 4-5 minute video to "hook" the participants and launch the small group discussion each week. A metaphor is embedded within each video to provide a unique means to consider the specific theme of each session. In addition to the imagery, the video contains an introduction or tie-in to the Scripture passage that will be studied. Finally, each video ends with a question to which group members will share their responses.

Video Discussion

This section provides questions to discuss immediately following the video presentation, to assist group members in considering the imagery, metaphors, and stories used in the video. These questions serve as meaningful segues into the Scripture and Discussion section that will follow.

Scripture and Discussion ~ 🖋

This is the most critical and constant component of each session. The session will focus on the Bible passages for that session that are included in the Participant Workbook. Each session will list a Scripture passage to be read aloud and then offer a variety of questions for review, reflection, and personal application.

Note that the sequence and number of questions is up to you and your group, and if desired you may decide to generate your own questions. Those completing the Participant Workbook will have read additional Scriptures during the week, and you are welcome to draw upon those selections to add to the study and discussion of the topic. Whichever questions you decide to use, you are strongly encouraged to include some of the questions with personal-application value that are listed toward the end of each section.

Closing

A closing prayer has been included for each session for those who wish to use it. You may choose to use the prayer listed simply as a resource or not at all. How your prayer is structured and offered is left to the discretion of you and your group. The prayer may be led by you, by another group member, or by the entire group. Sharing of joys and concerns should be included in the closing prayer.

Notes

A section of blank lines is provided at the end of each week's lesson. This space allows you to make notes that will assist you as you lead your small group. It can also be used to insert times, prayer requests, and other relevant information.

Week One

The Decision to Follow

The Decision to Follow

Preparing

The goal of this week's session is to remind people of our need to follow Christ's teaching and the example that he set for us. One way to learn about following Christ is to look at how his disciples followed him. Sometimes Jesus taught them with his words, through stories and parables. But at other times, Jesus simply asked his disciples to follow his example, to go where he went and to do as he did. They learned by being in his presence, and the more they were around him, the more they learned what he might do in the situations they encountered. That is still our call today. Disciples are called to follow Christ, and the only way we can do that well is by consistently being in God's presence.

The Scripture lesson from John 1 starts by using beautifully poetic language to describe how Jesus was the Word, God incarnate, come down to lead his people. Then John the Baptist predicts the Messiah's coming. Finally Jesus calls his first disciples, and they leave everything to follow him. The discussion questions for this week are designed to show how this chapter follows the early Christian path. First we recognize God in the world, then we hear about who God is, and finally we are called to follow God ourselves.

Just as in this week's video, the Christian walk is a journey. Sometimes it's an easy downhill stroll, but often it is punctuated with struggles and sudden changes. Use this imagery to help group members start talking with one another about how they came to know Christ and the kind of struggles and surprises they've faced along their journey.

Getting Started

Allow adequate time for introductions during the first week. Even if most of your group members are familiar with one another, using an icebreaker will strengthen connections and will be of great benefit to even one newcomer present. In addition to providing name tags for the group, consider choosing one of the following icebreakers or the conversation starter to let your group get to know one another and prepare for their group time together.

Icebreakers (choose one) – *index cards*

1. **Two True, One False:** Have all your group members write down three things about themselves. Two of the things must be true, and one must be false. Go around the room and have each person read his or her three things out loud. After each person reads the list, everyone else tries to guess which of the statements is false. This is a great way to learn fun facts about new people in your group.

2. **Detective:** Have your group members pair up. Give the pairs 5 minutes to find out three interesting things about each other. After the 5 minutes are up, have each of your "sleuths" present the three points of interest they learned. If you want to make it a competition, award one point for each interesting thing presented that no one else in the group knew.

3. **Can You Beat That?** Before your small group meets, write down a list of about twenty questions that people might compare about themselves, questions like "Who has traveled the furthest from here?" "Who has the coolest job?" "Who has read the longest book?" "Who has the most exotic pet?" and so on. Ask your group members each question. Whenever someone gives an answer, say, "Great, now who can beat that?" If there is any doubt about which answer is better, put it to a vote. Continue asking questions until everyone in your group has won at least once. (You may have to improvise questions to get everyone.)

Conversation Starter - ✱

Once introductions have been made, invite members in your group to share their response to this question: "What small-group experiences, if any, have you had in the past, and what do you hope to gain from participating in this small group?" Groups of eight or more should break into subgroups of 3-4 so that all may respond and still have time to complete the study session.

Logistics and Covenant

Depending upon whether you are a new or previously formed small group, the amount of time devoted to this portion of the study will vary. "How to Use This Leader Guide" suggests some information that may be appropriate here. Regardless of group history, all groups are encouraged to make a covenant with one another for this six-week study session.

Workbook Review - Next week.

This week's workbook readings focus on people in the Bible who were called to follow God. Have participants share what they wrote regarding their intention to follow Christ.

Read aloud John 1 as a group. Discuss what you would do if Jesus came today and asked you to leave everything and follow him.

Discussing

SHOW DVD VIDEO - Next week.

Video Discussion

In the video, Tom talks about the different times in our lives when God calls us to change how we are living. Ask your group members to give some examples of those times in their lives.

Tom mentions how Bible passages can encourage us in our journey. What Bible passages have been most important to your group members?

Scripture and Discussion

After you have read aloud from John 1, answer these questions:

1. In verse 1, John writes, "In the beginning was the Word." Who or what is he referring to, and why does he use this poetic imagery?

✝ 2. Throughout verses 4-9, John repeatedly refers to Jesus as "the light." What properties of light make it a good metaphor for Jesus? *Read* .

3. What did John the Baptist have to say about the Messiah in this passage?

4. Why did the Jewish leaders come out to question John the Baptist? What was the significance of this? *vs 23*

✝ 5. Why was John the Baptist baptizing people?

6. John calls Jesus "the Lamb of God." Why was this imagery significant for the Israelites?

7. What do you think Jesus told John's disciples when they "spent the day with him" that made them sure he was the Messiah?

✝ 8. Why did Jesus change Simon's name to Peter? What was significant about this change?

9. What was the response of all of the disciples Jesus told to follow him? (They followed, and they also told others to follow.)

10. Why did Nathanael think nothing good could come from Nazareth?

✝ 11. What does Jesus promise at the end of the reading? What does this mean, and what can we take from it today? *vs 50-51*

Closing

Invite group members to share joys and concerns about their week. Then close with the following prayer or with one of your own.

Lord Jesus, just as John proclaimed long ago, you are still God's Chosen One, and we exalt you as our ruler and guide. Teach us today to follow in your footsteps just as the disciples did. We come to you with many things on our hearts and minds. There are many things that distract us from your calling. But we ask, Lord, that you would remove the obstacles that keep us from following you, the challenges that the world puts in our way and the difficulties we bring upon ourselves when we are not obedient to your ways. We pray that you would help us follow you more closely, Jesus; and we ask that this week, you would help us to diligently study your word and put it into action in our lives. Please help us to grow in our faith; and as we grow, give us the courage to invite others to grow with us, both in this Bible study and in our every-day lives. We love you and thank you for all the blessings that you give and pray that you would keep us safe until we meet together again. Amen.

Notes

The Decision for a New Life

The Decision for a New Life

Preparing

The goal of this week's lesson is to show how important it is to find our new life in Jesus Christ. Nicodemus was at the apex of the Hebrew social structure, but he was drawn to Jesus' wisdom and truth. He understood that Jesus' teaching was not just for the poor and uneducated. It was a challenging, fulfilling lifestyle that could instruct even those who were highly educated religious leaders. Yet even this intellectual teacher of the law had difficulty understanding Jesus when he said that we must be "born again" into this new life. He did not understand the change Jesus was offering to people.

This was a hard lesson for Nicodemus because he was a very religious man. He was smart and respected and knew God's law. According to popular opinion, he was a great guy. But Jesus was saying that all those things weren't enough, that Nicodemus needed a new life to be a true follower of God. This lesson still resonates today. Many of your group members may be lifelong churchgoers. They are intelligent and may have been raised in the life of the church. Nicodemus teaches us that all of us, even the most knowledgeable, sometimes need a wake-up call to help us become like Jesus.

This week's video shows a man named William who heard God's call for new life in a dramatic way. Many people don't have such a dramatic story, but everyone can share something about how God has changed them. A key thread in William's story is his need for a decision for a new life. This week's discussion questions are designed to get your group talking about how God's new life has changed their lives.

Getting Started

Choose one of the following, either the icebreaker for active learners or the conversation starter for passive learners, as an introduction to your small-group time. This will allow members to connect with one another and shift their focus to this week's topic.

Icebreaker: Charade Relay

Before your small group meets, write down a list of twenty movies, TV shows, and books on index cards. When your group arrives, split them into two teams. When you say, "Go," have each team send a person to take a card from the pile. That person goes back to her or his team and tries to make them guess the word on the card through gestures and pantomime. NO SPEAKING! The person on the team who correctly guesses the word then takes a card from the pile and becomes the actor. Continue until one team has collected a set number of cards (depending upon your allotted time).

Conversation Starter

Ask your group members, "If you could live anywhere in the world and do any job you wanted, what would it be and why?" If time allows, let each person have a chance to discuss.

Workbook Review

This week's passages introduce us to people who were given new life. Have your group discuss how their own lives changed once they followed Christ.

As a group, read aloud John 3. Individually, compare yourselves to Nicodemus. How is your story like Nicodemus? How is it different?

Discussing

SHOW DVD VIDEO

Video Discussion

William had a pretty rough time in his early life. At what point on your journey have you been at your lowest? How did God build you up from that point?

William had several moments when his life suddenly changed. Looking back over your life, what moments do you see now that directly made you into the Christian you are today? *Do you care to share?*

Scripture and Discussion

After you have read aloud from John 3, answer these questions:

1. Who was Nicodemus, and what was his status among the Jews?

2. Why did Nicodemus come to see Jesus at night?

3. What did Jesus mean when he said that "no one can see the kingdom of God unless they are born again"?

4. What does it mean to be "born of water and the Spirit"?

5. Why does Jesus use the metaphor of the wind to represent the Holy Spirit?

6. What is the key to salvation, according to Jesus?

7. Why were John's disciples unhappy that Jesus and his disciples were baptizing?

8. Discuss in your own words what John the Baptist says about Jesus' divinity compared to John's humanity.

9. What does John's statement "He [Jesus] must become greater; I must become less" (verse 30) tell us about how we should live our lives today?

10. What does John teach us about eternal life in this passage?

Closing

Invite group members to share joys and concerns about their week. When everyone has shared, close with the following prayer or with one of your own:

Loving God, giver of eternal life, we praise you for
your power. Thank you for creating us and allowing

us the chance to get to know you, not as slaves but as children, grateful for the love of our Creator. Help us to crave that new life every day. Fill us with a longing for the things that make you happy, O God, and increase our desire to obey your commands. We admit our failures to you, Lord, and pray that you would forgive the sins that have separated us from you. In your strength, renew us each day into your eternal covenant and grant us the knowledge and grace to follow where you lead. Let our lives be a reflection of your glory so that we may shine like beacons of hope for those who still need to experience your new life. Give us the boldness to follow you and the wisdom to know what to say and do. We ask this through our glorious Savior, Jesus Christ, the only path to eternal salvation. Amen.

Notes

The Decision to Mature

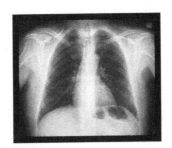

The Decision to Mature

Preparing

The goal of this week's session is to help participants see the connection between continual spiritual growth and the ability to perceive God's guidance in our life. Sometimes we Christians go to church on Sunday but live as we want for the rest of the week. We can become spiritually complacent. Jesus calls his followers to a richer experience in which we walk with him on our journey. He calls us to grow in our faith, to learn more about him, and to change our lives as we follow his example.

In this week's reading from John 4, Jesus talks to a Samaritan woman who knows about God but whose life is not consistent with her beliefs. Instead of getting angry at her disobedience, Jesus feels great compassion for her. He does not want to punish her but seeks to help her experience life as a faithful believer. He wants her belief to mature from simple knowledge to active faith. Jesus helps her to believe more fully, not only in him as the Messiah but in the promises that God made throughout Scripture. She responds joyfully to his teaching and essentially brings the whole village out to follow Jesus too. With the help of this week's questions, discuss with your group how God can use moments in each of our lives to mature us and help us grow in our walk with him.

This week's video also shows how God can use all kinds of situations to help us mature. We meet Chris, whose life has been turned upside-down by cancer. God has used his illness as a catalyst for change and maturity. Discuss what changes your group members have seen, or hope to see, in their lives as they mature in God.

Getting Started

Choose one of the following, either the icebreaker for active learners or the conversation starter for passive learners, as an introduction to your small-group time. This will allow members to connect with one another and shift their focus to this week's topic.

Icebreaker: Fuzzy Wuzzy

Give each member of your group an index card. Have each person write down: (1) the name of a childhood pet; (2) the name they gave a childhood stuffed animal/toy; and (3) their own childhood nickname. Collect the cards and read them one at a time while your group members try to guess which group member had which set of names. To make it a competition, you can give each correct guesser three points if they guess it on the pet's name, two points on the stuffed animal's name, and one point on the person's nickname.

Conversation Starter

What do you think is the hardest thing about growing up?

What part of your past do you miss the most, and what in the future are you most excited for?

Workbook Review

This week's Bible study focuses on people who had knowledge of God but were not necessarily putting it to use. As a result, God called them and brought things into their lives that enabled them to mature in their faith. Invite your group to share any Scripture or insight that struck them this week.

As a group, read aloud from John 4. Have your group answer this question: "In what ways do I, like the Samaritan woman, know about God but not follow as I should?"

Discussing

SHOW DVD VIDEO

Video Discussion

By God's grace, Chris has turned a potentially life-ending illness into a chance to grow closer to God and to his family. How do his actions inspire you?

As Chris asks, what would you change if you only had six months to live?

Scripture and Discussion

After you have read aloud from John 4, answer these questions:

1. What took Jesus to Samaria? Why was it strange for him to be there?

2. What was significant about Jacob's well? Why was it important to the Samaritans?

3. Why do you think Jesus asked the Samaritan woman for a drink? Was it more for her sake or for his?

4. Why didn't the Jews associate with the Samaritans? Why did Jesus ignore that expectation?

5. Originally, the woman just wanted "magic water" so she didn't have to fill her jar every day. What does this natural desire for the supernatural tell us about human nature in general and the Samaritan woman in particular?

6. Why does the Samaritan woman test Jesus when he reveals himself to be from God?

7. In what ways do we test God when he reveals himself to us in our everyday circumstances?

8. In what ways are Christians called to be harvesters in the world? How can we bring about this harvest?

9. What is the result of Jesus' talk with the Samaritan woman? Why is this such an important catalyst? (Jesus has come to save not only the Jews but all of God's children.)

10. Why does "a prophet have no honor in his own country"?

11. Why did Jesus refuse at first to heal the official's son?

Closing

Invite group members to share joys and concerns about their week. When everyone has shared, close with the following prayer or with one of your own:

Dear God, we thank you for the opportunity to learn about your incredible love. You are the only true God, and yet you came to earth to save us from our human failings and to lift us up from our mistakes. We find ourselves humbled by your love and ask that you would grant us pardon for our stumbling. Yet you don't ask us to stay in the place where you save us. You call us to grow and become more like you every day. Without you, this would be impossible, so we claim your provision and ask that you help us follow you more fully. Teach us where we need to grow, and mold our minds and spirits to be more accepting of your commands. Help us to be disciplined in our spiritual lives, to study your ways, and to live in your truth. Bless us with continued growth and help us bless others in our lives as our walk with you matures. Grant all these things, we pray, through your Holy Spirit. Amen.

Notes

Week Four

The Decision to Respond

Week Four

The Decision to Respond

Preparing

The goal of this week's lesson is to help people respond to God's calling in their lives. Sometimes it's hard to hear what God wants to say, and sometimes we just don't want to listen to what God is saying. God has given us gifts and abilities to do the will of Christ. The Holy Spirit is ready to guide their use. Only we, however, can put them to use.

In this week's reading of John 6, we see how Jesus used a boy's offering of his lunch to perform a great miracle. With a simple act of trust, God can do abundant things. But we have to be open to hearing what God wants, and often that means giving up something that we hold dear. Maybe it is a comfort that we can do without, or perhaps a sin that separates us from a truth God wants us to hear. We can't respond to God's call if we're not listening. But when we do hear the call, we must respond with the faith of a child—innocent and a little simple, yet life-changing.

In this week's video, we meet the Gaughans. Their young son read an article about an African boy in need of adoption, and he called on his family to heed God's calling. In responding to that call, the Gaughans not only blessed the life of the boy but received a blessing as well. With your group members, discuss times God blessed their lives when they responded to a calling. Also discuss why it is sometimes hard to hear God's voice and how they might improve in noticing opportunities to respond.

39

Getting Started

Choose one of the following, either the icebreaker for active learners or the conversation starter for passive learners, as an introduction to your small-group time. This will allow members to connect with one another and shift their focus to this week's topic.

Icebreaker: Telephone

Before the group meets, come up with a silly phrase, short enough to remember but long enough to be interesting (for example, "Fanny can't go dancing after eating bananas"). During your group, have participants sit in a circle or a line. Whisper the phrase into the first person's ear. They in turn will whisper it into the second person's ear, and so on until everyone has heard it. Have the last person announce what he or she heard and see if it is still the same phrase you started with. For added difficulty, do more than one phrase at a time.

Conversation Starter

What would you be willing to give up to:

1. get backstage passes to see your favorite band?

2. fly into space?

3. cure cancer?

4. feed an entire village of starving people?

5. save the life of one person you have never met?

Workbook Review

This week's readings focus on people God called to take action. Have your group discuss any Scriptures or insights they found particularly interesting this week.

Then have your group read aloud John 6. Give an example from your life of a time when God called you to do something. Describe the results you saw from following that call. Have others in the group give examples if they are comfortable doing so.

Discussing

SHOW DVD VIDEO

Video Discussion:

The Gaughans heard God's call through their young son. What has God's voice sounded like in your lives? What has it called you to do?

Often the hardest part of following God's call is taking the first step. What obstacles can get in the way of hearing and then heeding the call?

Scripture and Discussion

After you have read aloud from John 6, answer these questions:

1. Why did Jesus have such a large following with him?

2. Why do you think Jesus tested his disciples in this way?

3. What did the boy sacrifice by giving up his lunch? How was his sacrifice rewarded?

4. What do you think the disciples did with all the leftover food?

5. Why didn't Jesus allow the crowds to "make him king by force" (verse 15)?

6. Why were the disciples so afraid when they saw Jesus walking on the water?

7. Why did the crowd come to Jesus the second time?

8. How did Jesus turn their hunger for physical food into a hunger for spiritual sustenance?

9. In what different ways did the people of the crowd respond to Jesus' teaching?

10. Why didn't the people believe Jesus when he said that he was the Bread of Life and that they must eat of his body to attain eternal life? Why do people have trouble believing that today?

11. Why did so many disciples desert Jesus? Why did the Twelve stay with him?

Closing

Invite group members to share joys and concerns about their week. When everyone has shared, close with the following prayer or with one of your own:

Lord Jesus, we want to be like the twelve disciples. We want to be like the boy with the fish and the loaves. But so often, we are too scared or too embarrassed or too tired to follow your calling. Help us to be not only hearers of your word but also doers of your word. Quiet our hearts so that we may hear your calling in our lives. But when your calling does come, let us not shy away from it. Help us to be bold and go out into the world as your followers, sure in our cause and bolstered by the Holy Spirit. There are many things that stand in the way of your calling, God, but we ask that you would use us to move those obstacles. We will not sit idly by and wait for you to do the work. Let us instead be your hands and feet in the world. We thank you for the people in our lives who introduced us to this call, and we ask that you would use us to help further your light in this world. Forgive our insecurities and our frailty, Lord, and turn us into the active followers you desire. In the mighty name of Jesus Christ. Amen.

Notes

_____

_____

_____

_____

_____

_____

_____

_____

_____

_____

_____

_____

_____

_____

_____

_____

_____

_____

The Decision to Persevere

The Decision to Persevere

Preparing

The goal of this week's lesson is to remind us that following Jesus will almost certainly lead to hardships in life. When Jesus called his disciples to follow him, he did so with the full knowledge that somewhere in the future lay the cross. Jesus never promised that the road would be easy. In fact, he told his disciples that they would be hated because they followed him. In this week's reading from John 7, Jesus considers skipping the Festival of Booths. The Pharisees had heard about Jesus' preaching, that he called himself the Son of Man and claimed to be God. They assumed he would preach again at the festival and waited to catch him there. Jesus knew this in advance, yet he felt such a compassion for the people of Israel that he went to preach anyway. When he revealed himself, some people tried to capture him. This was Jesus' life, constantly on guard, but so filled with love for others that he would risk his life for their salvation. Following Christ will sometimes cause us to take risks as well.

In the video, we meet Nadeem. He was a Christian in Pakistan forced to flee because of his faith. He left behind a thriving business and friends and family because he shared his faith in Christ with a friend who chose to follow Jesus. Perhaps your group members do not face this kind of persecution. Still, they can probably think of times when being faithful to Christ's calling required risk and sacrifice. Nadeem risked his life so that his friend would know the joy of God's love and the salvation Christ offers. Discuss with your group what they feel called to risk to remain obedient to Christ.

Getting Started

Choose one of the following, either the icebreaker for active learners or the conversation starter for passive learners, as an introduction to your small-group time. This will allow participants to connect with one another and shift their focus to this week's topic.

Icebreaker: House of Cards

Bring several decks of cards to your group time. Separate your group into two teams (or more, depending on group size), and give each group a deck of cards. After you say "Go," give them 5 minutes to construct the biggest house of cards they can manage. All members of the teams must put at least one card on the house. Teams may NOT sabotage each others' building process, but collapses are still bound to occur. The biggest house at the end of 5 minutes wins.

Conversation Starter

What are some stories of Christian perseverance that you have heard? What is most inspiring about these stories?

Workbook Review

This week's readings are filled with stories of people who persevered through life's challenges for the sake of Christ. Have your group members present Scriptures and insights they found challenging and enlightening this week.

Then read John 7 aloud. This is a complicated passage on many levels. Discuss why Jesus chose to go to the festival incognito and yet decided to reveal his identity after he arrived and to start teaching.

Discussing

SHOW DVD VIDEO

Video Discussion

Nadeem knew what could happen if he brought his friend to Christ. How did he make the decision he did?

Be honest with yourself. How would you have dealt with the situation in which Nadeem found himself?

Scripture and Discussion

After you have read aloud from John 7, answer these questions:

1. Why did Jesus originally not want to go to the festival?

2. Why was it dangerous for Jesus to go into Judea? What persecution might have awaited him there?

3. What were some reasons different people at the festival might have been looking for Jesus?

4. Why did Jesus decide to reveal himself at the Temple?

5. What did Jesus talk about with the people in the Temple? What did he mean by it?

6. Imagine a preacher walking into your church one Sunday and saying the things that Jesus said. How do you think you would react?

7. Why didn't the crowd believe Jesus? What was their response to him?

8. What can we learn from the way the guards reacted to Jesus?

9. What was Nicodemus's reaction to the whole experience? How did his earlier experience with Christ affect his thought process?

10. This whole experience could have been avoided if Jesus had just not gone to the Festival. But he chose to go, so it must have been important to him. Why do you think Jesus went through this whole debacle? What was so important about it?

Closing

Invite group members to share joys and concerns about their week. When everyone has shared, close with the following prayer or with one of your own.

Precious Lord, you are our Refuge and our Strength.
We thank you for the great blessing that it is to be able

to meet together and worship you. Amidst the small difficulties of our lives, we sometimes forget the many whose struggles are far worse than our own. Thank you for the courage and strength you have given to the men and women who hold their ground against the darkness, around the world and throughout the ages. Help us, Father, never to forget those in need of our help and our prayers. We pray that you would continue to watch over your sheep who are in danger for their simple, profound trust in your Son, our Savior, Jesus Christ. We pray also for those in positions of power throughout the world, that their hearts would soften to the plight of Christians in their lands. Deliver us, Lord, from every evil, and grant us peace in our day . . . here and around the world. Amen.

Notes

The Decision to Surrender

Week Six

The Decision to Surrender

Preparing

The goal of this week's lesson is to bring attention to our need for God. We can't do everything on our own. Despite our best efforts, we will fail if we try to follow Christ without surrendering our will to him. In our reading of John 10 this week, Jesus refers to himself as "The Good Shepherd" who protects his sheep and leads them. Sheep were not particularly smart animals, often wandering off on their own and leaving the safety of the flock and the watchful eye of the shepherd. The sheep do not intentionally wander off to bad things. They simply forget the importance of being with the shepherd. When we try to live at a distance from Christ, we enter into uncertain and even dangerous territory. It would be absurd for a sheep to lead the shepherd around, yet that is what we do when we forget to look to Jesus for direction. As the Good Shepherd, Jesus wants to lead us to green pastures and protect us from the dangers of this world, but we have to go where he leads and listen to his voice to make it possible. The key is continuous surrender to God's will, no matter where we are being led.

In the video, we find a young woman named Whitney who developed a plan to serve the Lord in Africa, sensing God's call to help people there. Yet when she got there, everything seemed to go wrong. Her plan began to collapse, and she learned again how to listen for God's direction and to follow. As this Bible study ends, discuss with your group the plans they have for their spiritual lives and what plans God may have for them as they go forward.

Getting Started

Choose one of the following, either the icebreaker for active learners or the conversation starter for passive learners, as an introduction to your small-group time. This will allow members to connect with one another and shift their focus to this week's topic.

Icebreaker: Trust Fall

Clear a large space where your group members can stand. Have one member stand with his or her back to the other members. This will be the "Trust Faller." Have several members link arms behind the Trust Faller so that they can catch the faller. Make sure that the catchers are paying attention and are physically capable of catching the Faller. On the count of three, the Trust Faller will fall backward (without looking) into the waiting arms of the catchers. Repeat this with each member of the group.

Conversation Starter

What are some things that many people find hard to give up? What is the hardest thing that you feel called to give up?

Workbook Review

This week's readings talk about people who trusted God enough to surrender their lives to God's will, despite physical and social struggles. Ask your group members to share any insights or Scriptures that moved them this week.

Read aloud John 10. Discuss what it means to be totally dependent on someone and how that dependence should shape us in humility and trust in God's leading. Give an example of someone you have depended on and ask the group members to do likewise.

Discussing

Video Discussion

What are some things that Whitney surrendered to follow God's call to Africa?

Why do you think God allowed obstacles to impede Whitney's plan, even though it was something to which God had called her?

Scripture and Discussion

Read aloud from John 10 and answer these questions:

1. What are some reasons Jesus uses the imagery of sheep to represent people?

2. Why are the Pharisees considered "thieves and robbers" by Jesus?

3. Both Jesus and his "sheep" have to surrender in this passage. In what way did Jesus surrender of himself? In what ways must the sheep surrender to his will?

4. Who do you think Jesus is referring to when he talks about the hired hand? Who is the wolf?

5. Does the voice of God change from situation to situation? Why or why not?

6. What are some ways you have heard the voice of God in your life? What has God sounded like to you?

7. What were people saying about Jesus when he made these claims? Why were they divided about him?

8. When they ask Jesus to claim his Messiahship plainly, why doesn't he just say, "I am the Messiah"?

9. What parts of Jesus' speech seem most striking to you? What parts are most convicting or convincing?

10. The Bible simply says that when the crowd turned on him, Jesus "escaped their grasp." How do you think Jesus actually got free of the angry mob?

11. What can we learn from the people who followed Jesus across the Jordan at the end of this passage?

Closing

Invite group members to share joys and concerns about their week. When everyone has shared, close with the following prayer or with one of your own:

Creator and Redeemer, we claim you as the Good Shepherd in our lives. We thank you for calling us to follow you. We praise you for teaching us gently, for leading us wisely, and for correcting us with your guiding staff when we need it. Help us, we pray, to stay on the path you have marked out for us, and save us from the thieves and the robbers who seek to steal our salvation and destroy our will to follow you. Lord, we surrender our plans and our purpose to you, because we freely admit that your ways are better than our own. We are so ready to go astray and to follow our own desires. Search for us, Father, and point us back to the narrow path. Give us the courage to surrender and the character to call others to do likewise. You are the Wise Counselor and the Good Shepherd, and we love and praise you, Father, Son, and Holy Spirit. And now we pray together the prayer shared by the church throughout the centuries:

> *Our Father, who art in heaven, hallowed be thy name.*
> *Thy kingdom come, thy will be done, on earth as it is*
>   *in heaven.*
> *Give us this day our daily bread,*
> *and forgive us our trespasses,*
> *as we forgive those who trespass against us.*
> *And lead us not into temptation, but deliver us from evil.*
> *For thine is the kingdom and the power and the glory*
>   *forever.*
> *Amen.*

Notes

Notes

_____

_____

_____

_____

_____

_____

_____

_____

_____

_____

_____

_____

_____

_____

_____

_____

_____

_____

_____

_____

Notes

CPSIA information can be obtained
at www.ICGtesting.com
Printed in the USA
LVHW08s2145190818
587474LV00033B/492/P